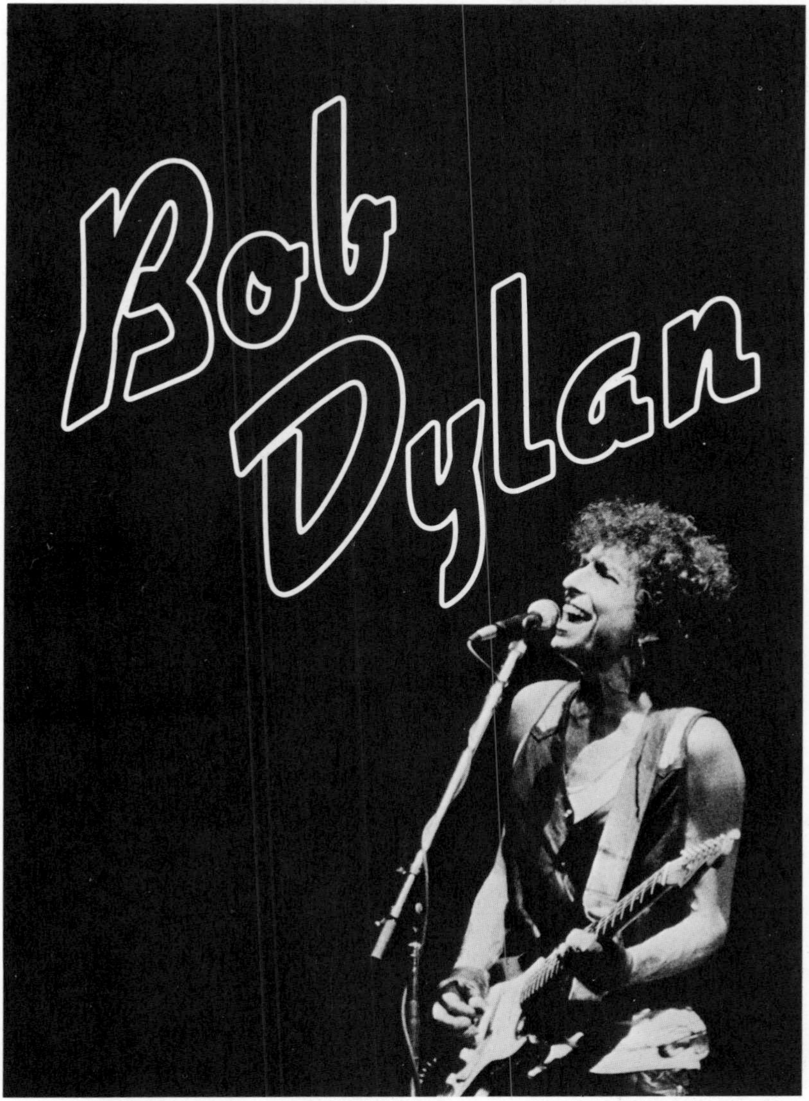
Bob Dylan

Bob Dylan

Spellbinding Songwriter

Nathan Aaseng

Lerner Publications Company ■ Minneapolis

PHOTO CREDITS:

John Rott, News-Tribune & Herald, Duluth, MN, pp. 1, 44; Arthur D'Amario III/Retna Ltd., p. 2; © Elliott Landy 1968/Retna Ltd., p. 6; Museum of Modern Art/Film Stills Archive, pp. 9, 39; Lester Cohen/ASCAP, p. 10; Independent Picture Service, pp. 12, 24; Theatre Collection, Museum of the City of New York, p. 14; Jeff Syme, pp. 17, 18; Courtesy of Hibbing High School, p. 19 (left and right); NMN Inc., p. 19 (center); Used by permission of Woody Guthrie Publications Inc., p. 21; Newport Daily News, p. 26; UPI/Bettman Newsphotos, p. 28; Bowling Green State University Music Library, pp. 31, 41; Movie Star News, p. 32; Chris Walter/Retna Ltd., p. 33; Henry Diltz/USA for Africa, p. 38; Robert Matheu/Retna Ltd., p. 42; Minnesota Historical Society, p. 46; Greg Helgeson, p. 47; Gary Gershoff/Retna Ltd., p. 49

Front cover photograph by Ross Barnett/London Features International/USA Ltd
Back cover photograph by John Rott, News-Tribune & Herald, Duluth, MN

LIBRARY OF CONGRESS CATALOGING-IN-PUBLICATION DATA

Aaseng, Nathan.
  Bob Dylan, spellbinding songwriter.

  (The Achievers)
  Summary: Examines the life, career, and music of the influential singer-songwriter who has made significant contributions to the field of folk music and rock and roll.
  1. Dylan, Bob, 1941-   —Juvenile literature. 2. Rock musicians—United States—Biography—Juvenile literature. [1. Dylan, Bob, 1941-   . 2. Musicians] I. Title. II. Series.
  ML3930.D97A65   1987   784.4'924 [B] [92]   86-27714
  ISBN 0-8225-0489-8 (lib. bdg.)

Manufactured in the United States of America

International Standard Book Number: 0-8225-0489-8
Library of Congress Catalog Card Number: 86-27714

1 2 3 4 5 6 7 8 9 10 97 96 95 94 93 92 91 90 89 88 87

Contents

Blowin' in the Wind

A thin singer with tousled hair and a scowl stepped onto a stage at a New York coffeehouse. A harmonica was rigged around his neck so that it hung near his mouth, and he carried a guitar in his hand. He called himself Bob Dylan. His odd appearance probably caused a few heads to turn at this early 1960s performance. In his beat-up blue jeans and workshirt, Bob looked as though he had stepped right out of bed onto the stage.

Dylan started to sing. It was not a pleasant sound nor even very musical. But Bob sang with such energy and honesty that people listened to him. He sang his own songs about the topics of the day that were troubling many people. This was a time when America was caught up in a whirl of protest and change. Civil rights, war, violence, and the restlessness of young adults seemed to take over the headlines. Bob Dylan put the feelings of many people, especially young people, into words and music. Even at the beginning, his songs were filled with fascinating word pictures and touched a range of emotions that went far beyond the usual "I love you, do-wah" rock lyrics.

Bob Dylan isn't a typical music superstar like the ones who appear on MTV today. He isn't flashy, or loud, nor is he comfortable with all of the electronic gadgets of the recording studio. The era of slick, processed videos seems to have passed him by. He doesn't even plan recording dates in advance, and he rarely tries to smooth over errors with extra takes in a recording studio because "my stuff is based on wrong things." He can sound like a typical older generation nag when he complains that "nobody's telling kids anything through music anymore."

Acts come and go in the music business, and big stars can fade overnight. But even if Dylan were to disappear tomorrow, he would still have more influence on popular music than any of the current hottest groups. Bruce Springsteen is known as "The Boss," but much of his inspiration came from Dylan. When asked what musicians they learned the most from, the Beatles listed Bob Dylan. Dozens of other popular groups over the past two decades can say the same.

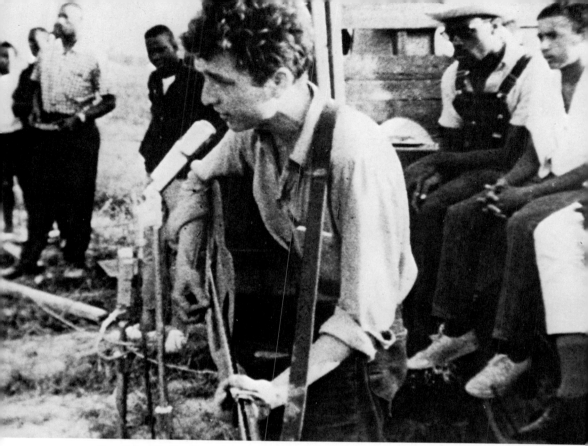

Don't Look Back, a documentary made during Bob's 1965 concert tour of Britain, contains this scene, in which Bob played at a concert for civil rights in Mississippi in 1963.

Dylan touched so many nerves that he inspired roughly sixty recorded versions of one of his songs, "Blowin' in the Wind," and in a single month triggered forty-eight different recordings of his songs by popular performers.

Sociologists talk about how Dylan has changed our

In March 1986 Bob Dylan was presented the American Society of Composers, Authors and Publishers (ASCAP) Founders Award. The award was presented "to Bob Dylan whose legendary contributions have been a sustaining influence on the music of an entire generation."

culture. Politicians quote him in speeches. Professors teach college courses about his poetry. He is considered the most important writer of popular songs of the past three decades. Magazines have called him the spokesman for a whole new generation of Americans.

Bob Dylan is a mystery, a fascinating puzzle, who has probably received more praise and criticism than any other musician of his time.

When Dylan's fame began to grow, there was a rush to find out more about this singer with the raspy

10

voice. Interviewing Dylan was like trying to interview some mysterious person from ancient times. The young man in the blue jeans would give no hints as to who he really was.

Reporters found that talking to Dylan generally added more confusion than it cleared up. He pretended he did not know what they were talking about, and teased them with long, nonsensical stories. The press would be eagerly taking notes until they finally realized Bob was making the whole thing up. When explaining how he became a rock star, Bob spun a wild story that included a series of burned houses, knifings, and a temporary job as a Chinaman. Editors dreaded trying to edit Dylan interviews to fit their publications, because they didn't understand enough of what he was saying to know what was important and what wasn't.

There were so many stories and rumors about Dylan, many of them started by Bob himself, that it was hard to sift out the facts. After all these years, no one really knows why he changed his last name from Zimmerman to Dylan. Was it because he enjoyed the works of the poet Dylan Thomas or the heroism of Sheriff Matt Dillon on the TV series *Gunsmoke*? Was it after some relative of his? Or was there some other reason? When writers complained that Dylan was uncooperative, he would disagree and tell them that they were simply asking the wrong questions.

THE FOLKLORE CENTER

Presents

BOB DYLAN

IN HIS FIRST NEW YORK CONCERT

SAT. NOV. 4, 1961   8:40pm

CARNEGIE CHAPTER HALL

154 WEST 57th STREET • NEW YORK CITY

All seats $2.00

Tickets available at: The Folklore Center
                             110 MacDougal Street
GR 7 - 5987   New York City 12, New York

                             or at door

Even his most devoted fans were often baffled by his behavior. Part of the reason for the confusion was that Dylan was determined to be himself. He saw no reason why he should give the answers a typical entertainment star is expected to give. In fact, he refused to be typical of anything. This made it even more difficult to answer the question, "Who is Bob Dylan?"

Left, this flyer advertised Dylan's first New York concert. He had already been signed by Columbia Records, but only about fifty people showed up for the concert — mostly friends of Bob's.

Dylan looks very young in this shot of him in a recording studio in the early 1960s.

Like a Rolling Stone

Robert Allen Zimmerman was born on May 24, 1941, in Duluth, Minnesota. He was his parents' first child.

When Bob was seven, his father quit his job after contracting polio and moved the family to Hibbing, Minnesota. The Zimmermans settled there permanently, and Bob was brought up in a stable family, in a Jewish household. His father, Abraham, did very well in business as an appliance dealer. Mr. Zimmerman's witty sense of humor rubbed off on Bob. Bob's mother, Beatty, was an intelligent, talkative woman. Apparently the talkative trait was not passed on to her son.

Bob was a skinny kid, but that did not stop him from helping his father by hauling refrigerators and washers.

He delivered the heaviest appliances as easily as boys larger than he.

While working with his father, Bob learned some sobering lessons about life. Hibbing had once been a booming mining community, but the rich supply of iron ore in the open-pit mines could not hold out forever. Most of the people worked for the mines, and the town of about 18,000 suffered some rough times when its main industry slowed down. Once, Mr. Zimmerman took Bob to a poor section of town. He assigned his son the task of collecting money from customers who were behind in their payments. He wanted Bob to see that there was another side to life besides the comfortable style the Zimmermans were growing used to.

It was an experience that Bob could not forget. Many of the people he found were deeply in debt. They simply could not pay and had little hope that things could get better. Bob could not help but ask himself why some people's lives were full of such sorrow. As the years went by, he always kept an eye open for the poor, the uneducated, and the powerless.

Bob did not run around with a large group of friends. He kept to himself most of the time, and started recording his thoughts on paper at the age of eight. Within a few years he had written a large collection of poems. While his interest in poetry grew, he also felt drawn toward music. One day Mr. Zimmerman brought home a surprise for the family. He had bought a piano. At first, Bob sat down eagerly at the piano bench, excited about learning to play. But the ten-year-old boy was not patient enough to follow the lesson plans. It seemed to him that it would take forever before he could play songs he liked. After one lesson he gave up in frustration and left the instrument to his five-year-old brother, David.

The Zimmerman family house in Hibbing

Because David stayed with his lessons, he was thought of as the musical one in the family. But Bob began to learn music on his own. At his own pace, he taught himself what he wanted to know about the guitar, piano, and harmonica. He also studied any singer or musician who came to town, and haunted the local record store listening for new sounds.

This is the synagogue Bob attended as long as he lived in Hibbing.

Bob Zimmerman looked like a juvenile delinquent in his junior year, *upper left*, but had cleaned up for his senior yearbook photo, *lower right*. Hibbing High School, *center*, was a large, beautiful building.

As a teenager, Bob began to feel that the small-town life of Hibbing was not for him. The restless youngster was eager to get out on his own in the world. He talked his father into buying him a motorcycle so he could take off for Minneapolis or Duluth on the weekend. He spent as much time as he could away from Hibbing, listening to music down in Minneapolis or meeting musicians in St. Paul. Even with these wanderings,

19

Bob had little trouble keeping up with his schoolwork. He graduated from Hibbing High School along with the rest of his class in 1959.

From there, Bob traveled downstate to Minneapolis. He found a college fraternity house to stay in and attended the University of Minnesota for about six months. He later claimed that he left school rather than carry out a biology assignment that involved killing an animal.

At this time, coffeehouses were popular gathering spots for young people. These were mostly plain, no-frills, inexpensive places where people could sit and talk and listen to live music. Bob found a job playing at a coffeehouse for two dollars a night.

Although he enjoyed many kinds of music, including rock 'n' roll, Bob became a folksinger. It was an easy style for a young man like Dylan, because a person did not have to be rich to be a folksinger. Folksingers usually played alone with only their guitars to accompany them. They often sang simple tunes about people or events from their country's past. As a folksinger, Bob could try out his own music without having to rely on a band to practice and play with him.

One of the musicians Bob had grown to admire most was a man named Woody Guthrie. The Oklahoma-born Guthrie has been called America's top folk song writer in this century. Although many of his songs, such as

"This Land is Your Land," became widely known, Guthrie never won the kind of fame that musicians receive today. Bob, who had now changed his name to Dylan, heard that the great folksinger was lying

Bob visited his idol, Woody Guthrie, as often as he could when he first came to New York. Here Guthrie posed with his guitar in a photograph taken years before Dylan met him.

21

in a hospital in New Jersey. Guthrie was in the middle of a long battle with an illness called Huntington's disease. Dylan decided he would visit Guthrie and he left for New York in 1961. He visited Guthrie many times while he stayed in New York, and met many other popular folksingers who were Guthrie's friends. Because of Woody's illness, he and Bob were not able to talk much, but Guthrie's music got through to the twenty-year-old Dylan.

In these early days in New York, Bob was sort of a misfit. He drifted into a section of the city known as Greenwich Village. He made some friends almost immediately who let him sleep in their apartments.

Even among the hodgepodge of artists who lived in Greenwich Village, Bob stood out as unusual. He seemed like a shy, stubborn, small-town boy who had somehow stumbled into the largest city in the country. But Bob had a way of getting people to notice him when it came to music. He had an easy sense of humor and was not afraid to try spur-of-the-moment ideas in the middle of a performance. There was nothing phony about his actions on stage. His music was straightforward and his harsh voice drew attention to the words, not the tune, of his songs.

Many talented young performers have had their dreams shattered in New York, and Dylan could easily have been another. He might have shuffled through coffeehouses in New York for years were it not for some good breaks. The first one came when a *New York Times* reporter sat in on a Dylan performance. The reporter watched as Dylan's poetic songs put the audience in a thoughtful mood for a while, then his easy humor and sudden inspirations pulled them out of it until they were all laughing. The *Times* reporter enjoyed the performance so much that he wrote a glowing review of this unexpected find. Since the *New York Times* is one of the major newspapers on the East Coast of the United States, many people read about this new singer.

At about the same time, Bob made other important contacts. A talent scout for the Columbia Record Company was checking on a new recording personality named Carolyn Hester. Dylan played harmonica on Hester's record, and the talent scout found him fascinating. The scout did not even have to hear Bob perform his own music to know that he was something special. He signed Dylan to a contract with the record company.

Dylan's songs about racial injustice won the heart of Joan Baez. Joan, who was the same age as Bob, liked the way that Bob could sing about the very things she was feeling. As the leading female folksinger in the United States, her backing was important for Dylan. The two became close friends during the 1960s,

Joan Baez was the most popular female folksinger in the United States when she met Dylan.

and she offered him her help for his career, even asking him to join her in concerts.

Bob was also lucky to find a good manager. Albert Grossman, a fairly conservative businessman, joined up with Dylan early in Bob's career. The manager was able to keep Bob's finances in order without crowding in on his life.

Even with this help, Bob's first album hardly shook the world. The album, entitled simply *Bob Dylan,* was an ordinary collection of folk songs and blues. Few of them were Dylan's songs. The critics paid little attention to it when it was released in 1962 and few people went out of their way to buy it.

Oddly enough, Dylan's success depended on another group's record. Peter, Paul and Mary was one of the more popular singing groups in the country. When they recorded Dylan's song, "Blowin' in the Wind," his words were spread throughout the country. The song asked questions about life, war, and prejudice. It made people stop and think. The song became such a hit that it made superstars of both the singers and the songwriter. It didn't hurt that when Peter, Paul and Mary sang the song in concert, they always introduced it as having been "written by the most important folk artist in America today, Bob Dylan."

Dylan's next albums were *The Freewheelin' Bob Dylan* and *The Times They Are A-Changin'.* In these

At the 1963 Newport Folk Festival in Newport, Rhode Island, Dylan sang with the superstars of folk music. To the left of Dylan are Peter Yarrow, Mary Travers, and Paul Stookey (Peter, Paul and Mary), and Joan Baez. The Freedom Singers are behind Dylan, and Pete Seeger is to the right. Dylan accompanied their singing with the trademark harmonica around his neck and his acoustic guitar.

albums, Bob spoke of changes that would sweep the world. In songs such as "A Hard Rain's A-Gonna Fall," he gave warnings about the future. In some ways, he seemed like an ancient prophet who had come to try to get people to change their evil ways.

Most of his songs were what he described as flashes of images. Even if their meaning is not clear, they paint pictures in the listener's mind. Because of his special gift with words and his vision, Dylan was labeled the finest young poet in the United States by some reviewers and fans. Of course, there were also language experts who claimed that Bob did not know the first thing about poetry.

Although the "protest singer" had won thousands of fans, there were probably almost as many music lovers who were disgusted by him. Experts laughed at Bob's harsh voice and questioned what he knew about music. His tunes were often so simple that even a beginning guitarist could play them with no problem. People close to Dylan claim that he is really a much more skilled guitarist than he seems in concerts or on records. It is just that he prefers not to have the music take attention away from the words.

When Bob cried out that the times were changing, it scared many people. To those who liked their lives just the way they were, Dylan seemed to be nothing more than an angry, undisciplined rebel. But whether they liked it or not, Dylan was right. The times were changing, especially in the mid-1960s. Summer riots destroyed many city blocks. Protest marches, peace rallies, and the civil rights movement swept through the land. Dylan seemed to be in the middle of all the noise. He performed at special concerts to raise money for people active in these issues. Once he took a trip

27

Hundreds of thousands turned out for the 1963 March on Washington in support of civil rights. Dylan was there, and played a little music with Joan Baez and Paul Stookey.

to the Deep South to play at a song festival for black voting rights. Dylan paid his own way and performed for free. To the young and to older people concerned with justice and the rights of the common person, Dylan was a hero.

It's All Over Now, Baby Blue

Bob Dylan, however, didn't feel he was born to be a hero. His fans found him confusing. Although he was often an easy-going, cooperative person who did not like to hold grudges, Dylan seemed to avoid people. Once, an organization that admired Bob's work brought him to a fancy dinner to honor him. It was a mistake. Bob felt totally out of place at the formal, dressed-up affair. When he finally stood up to give an acceptance speech, Dylan had everyone squirming in their seats. He was not one to say the proper, polite things expected of him. By the time he finished saying what was on his mind, much of the audience was offended. Such experiences probably persuaded Dylan to avoid all but a small circle of friends.

Dylan disturbed his followers even more by starting to write more love songs and personal songs and fewer political songs. Not only did he stay away from politics and civil rights, he claimed he had never wanted to be a political or protest singer. "Don't follow anything" was his motto, and just as he refused to follow others, he refused to lead. He said he was only concerned with individuals, and had no time for groups or causes. His young fans may have been disappointed that Bob would not be their spokesman. He said his songs were not written to give advice; they were just songs about the way he saw things.

By 1965, Dylan's songs were less about the troubled world and more about his own troubled self, and they began to reach a wider audience. The Byrds' version of "Mr. Tambourine Man" actually brought more fame to the composer, Dylan, than it did to those who performed it.

That year Dylan took his guitar and harmonica on a European tour. His fame abroad was at least as great as it was at home. At one time, five of Dylan's albums were ranked in the top twenty in England! But in spite of the mobs of howling fans, Dylan grew bored of standing up and singing songs the same way every night during his tour. It all seemed too easy for him. The audience may have loved it, but Dylan knew that he could not go on that way. By the end of

Joan Baez and Bob Dylan enjoy a joke together. Joan went with Bob on his 1965 tour of Britain, but they had a falling-out during the tour and didn't play together again until 1974.

the tour, even the standing ovations he received did not cheer him. He had to move on to something else in music or quit playing. The times were still changing and so was Dylan. He had to find some way to break out of the pattern he was in.

One day, Bob sat down and started to write a poem about hatred. Once he started, the words flowed out of him. The poem changed and became more about

Dylan created a whole new image of himself when he began to record and perform with an electric guitar and a band.

freedom and being on your own. It rambled on for ten full pages. Dylan did not think it was a song at first, but later the words came across to him in a rhythm. He cut the poem down to size and put it to music. Dylan had prepared a song that became a hit in a new field, rock 'n' roll. "Like a Rolling Stone" signaled a change in Dylan and another break from the labels that were put on him.

When Bob returned to Britain in 1969 for his first concert since his motorcycle accident, he came back in short hair and with his acoustic guitar. He also played some rock 'n' roll numbers.

At the Newport Folk Festival of 1965, a crowd of Dylan fans squeezed together to hear the easy folk style of their hero. To their shock, Bob brought out a *band* and *electric* guitars. Dylan, the folksinger, with a band, and electric guitars! To his fans, it seemed that Bob had sold out, that he was giving up serious music for the money-making world of rock 'n' roll. He was starting to perform *noise* instead of meaningful songs, they thought. As he played and sang, the shouts and boos from the audience grew louder until Dylan walked off stage. Some of those backstage thought that he had tears in his eyes. When he was finally talked into returning to the stage, Bob closed the show with a number called "It's All Over Now, Baby Blue." It seemed to be his farewell to the old Dylan.

For a while he had to battle boos at other concerts. But Bob insisted that his songs needed a band and more sound to make them complete. In the end, he won far more fans than he lost. Within months after entering the field of rock music, Dylan soared to the top of the top forty charts. He was either recording or touring, reaching new fans everywhere.

The rich and glamorous world of rock 'n' roll did not change him, he changed it. He introduced a new type of song that some later called "folk rock." In this, he blended the sounds of rock with the word-pictures of folk music. Bob helped demonstrate that rock music could be more than just cute phrases and nonsense refrains, it could also be played with meaningful and mystical words. Before long, hundreds of imitators sang and wrote songs patterned after Dylan's.

In 1966 Dylan was cruising around on his motorcycle. It was an ordinary trip through the countryside near his home in Woodstock, New York, just like many Bob had enjoyed in past years. A life of fame and fortune did not stop him from traveling around the country, looking for experiences on the backroads and in the poolrooms of small towns. From these trips, Bob gained the background for realistic stories of people. When he was on the road, he could write songs while sitting alone in a motel room or in the back of a taxi. But on this trip, Dylan almost lost his life. The back wheel of his motorcycle locked and Dylan was thrown off the bike at high speed. His neck was broken and deep cuts were slashed across his head.

The newspapers found out nothing about it from Dylan. All sorts of rumors started to explain why Bob was no longer seen in public. Some heard of the accident and guessed that he was crippled or dead. Slowly and quietly Bob Dylan recovered from his injuries, but the narrow escape had its effect on him. He avoided the spotlight more than ever. He slowed down the frightful pace of recording and performing. He stayed away from concerts completely and did not put out his next album until 1968.

When he finally returned to the recording studio, his album *John Wesley Harding* again showed that Dylan was not interested in following the latest trends in music. While others turned to louder, more electric sounds or were influenced by music from East Asia, Bob went his own way. He turned out a softer sound, closer to his folk roots.

Long-haired, leather-clad, electrified Bob Dylan in the late 1970s

He surprised his fans again by drifting into the area of country music in his next album, *Nashville Skyline.* All of a sudden, the long-haired protester of the new generation was playing alongside old favorites like Johnny Cash. What was Dylan up to? As usual, the music critics had fun blasting Dylan's latest switch.

Those who knew Dylan, though, knew that he had not gone completely conservative. It was just another sign that Bob Dylan was always on the lookout for new ways to make music.

In 1971, a series of natural disasters caused a terrible famine in the Asian country of Bangladesh. George Harrison, a former member of the Beatles, wanted to do something to help the suffering people. He put together a concert of top rock musicians. All of them performed for no charge so the money they raised could be sent to the people of Bangladesh.

In the middle of the concert, a familiar face appeared on the stage, dressed in the blue denim jeans and workshirt of his beginning days in New York. The shouts and applause for Bob Dylan were deafening. Dylan sang many of his old hits. Blowing his harmonica while strumming his acoustic guitar, he treated the crowd to memories of old times. Again, Bob had done the unexpected.

By the early 1970s, people should not have been surprised by anything that Dylan tried. He headed

Dylan's commitment to helping others continues. He joined in the recording session of "We Are the World" for USA for Africa. Bob is second from the right in the second row.

for Hollywood, of all places, in 1973. Not only did he write and sing the music for the movie, *Pat Garrett and Billy the Kid,* he also acted in it. Among his many other projects were a movie of his own making, a book he was writing, and a special on television. None of this brought kind words from the critics.

Baffled by Dylan and his lack of communication, all they could do was guess that Dylan was constantly "reinventing himself" just to be different.

Another "reinvention" appeared in 1974, when

Bob Dylan in character and in costume as "Alias," his role in *Pat Garrett and Billy the Kid.*

Dylan broke an eight-year absence from the concert tour. Of course, he did it in an unusual fashion. He gathered a collection of top entertainers, including Joan Baez, Joni Mitchell, and Roger McGuinn of the Byrds, as well as some lesser-known poets and musicians. They went on the road together in what was called the "Rolling Thunder Revue."

In the late 1970s, Bob made an album every year. His usual method of recording shows his carefree, some say "lazy," approach to work. There was no set schedule of recording dates for Bob. He just showed up at the studio with some musicians when he had songs that were ready to record. Friends often joined him at the studio and enjoyed a quiet party while watching him play. Dylan did not care to have things planned to the last detail. Rather than rehearse a song to perfection, Bob often recorded only one or two takes of a song. As a result, some of his recordings are unpolished. But Bob liked things to happen naturally or not at all.

For those who thought they had seen just about everything from Bob Dylan, 1979 was another startling jolt. Dylan had been receiving criticism for his latest work. He had been touring with backup singers and a bigger band which included a saxophone and a flute. Music fans complained that the once-refreshing Dylan was now imitating Las Vegas entertainers with

For the "Rolling Thunder Revue" tour, Dylan wore a large hat.

an artificial polish, the very kind of phoniness he'd always scorned. Just when they were convinced that Dylan was now in music only for the money, Bob suddenly appeared at concerts wearing a cross around his neck. Once scornful of organized churches, Dylan

Bob, *left*, continues to move with the times. He enlisted Dave
Stewart of Eurythmics, *right*, to help with a video for one of his
songs.

seemed to have been converted into an old-time religion
singer. Even those who had come to expect the
unexpected from him found this hard to believe. Some
fans booed, some walked out of his concerts, some
just sat in silence as Dylan sang his new songs. "Don't
look back," Dylan told his audiences.

42

Dylan wasn't through with his chameleon changes yet, though. In 1985, he joined the world of high-tech sound with his *Empire Burlesque* album. Was there anything Dylan wouldn't try? Was there any sense to this moving target named Bob Dylan or was it simply that he hated the idea of settling into any pattern at all?

Dylan finally provided some clues to his career with the release of his *Biograph* album in 1985. An arranged collection of songs from his past, the album contained a book that was crammed with Bob's own notations about the different songs. Looking back over this sample of more than two decades of success—fifty-three songs that barely scratched the surface of his career—it was possible to get a view of this man. But *Biograph* provided only a few glimpses; anyone looking for easy answers would still give up in confusion.

Bob played with Tom Petty, *left,* on his 1986 tour.

You Gotta Serve Somebody

Does Bob Dylan enjoy wrapping himself in mystery and chaos just to throw everybody off his trail? The answer comes in two parts. First, it is true that Dylan hates being typecast. He feels that labels are restrictions placed on him by people who want to control him. He snarls at some of the more complimentary descriptions of him. Calling him a modern-day prophet or a sage, a protester or a folksinger, a country boy or a rock singer, puts him in a box. Protesters don't hole up for years like hermits, folksingers don't flail away on electric guitars, country boys don't join up with Hollywood, outlaws don't study the Bible. Dylan wants to do all the things those different roles allow. At the risk of losing his fans and of being told he is always reinventing his image, Dylan goes his own way.

45

As a result, Dylan's path has been a complicated one. Nowhere is that more obvious than in his family life. Does he like a normal family life or not? He was both a free-spirited rebel and an average family man, at different times. He used to claim that he did not even know where his parents were, that he was an orphan, yet he once brought them to New York to

Dylan has come a long way from Hibbing. This is Howard, the main street, in the 1950s. The Zimmermans' appliance store is just off this street, on Fifth Avenue.

Dylan showed up in St. Paul, Minnesota, for the graduation of his step-daughter, Maria, from Macalester College in 1986. He sat on the grass with his brother David and ex-wife Sara. He sneaked in quietly and unannounced, but, dressed in a wool hat, leather jacket, and heavy boots in 80-degree weather, he still managed to call attention to himself.

see him in concert at Carnegie Hall, and he is protective of his father, who has passed away.

Few people can do so much in the entertainment world while keeping their lives so completely out of the news. Bob was quietly married to Sara Lowndes for many years. The couple had five children in their marriage, but even many of his fans were unaware of his family life. Many believe that some of Bob's best love songs were written for Sara, although the two were later divorced. Bob once half-seriously asked his wife to hide in the closet when a reporter came to interview him. Although he did not really go that far, he was skilled at keeping reporters away from his family.

Bob Dylan spends a good deal of time now on a farm that he owns just outside of the metropolitan area of Minneapolis-St. Paul, Minnesota. In many ways he is not much different from the average American approaching middle age.

The second part of the answer to the question of why Dylan seemed to keep changing was given by Dylan himself. He once said, "I like to stay part of that stuff that don't change." Despite the many phases that his career has passed through, something has stayed the same about Bob Dylan. His involvement in the campaign for black voting rights in 1962, his appearance at the concert for Bangladesh in 1971, and his performances at the Live Aid concert and on USA for Africa's "We Are The World" come from an enduring part of his character. In homage to his small-town midwestern roots, he even conceived of the Farm Aid concert to help United States farmers.

Perhaps the best way to explain Dylan is to say that he is not interested in being either an average person or a hero. Dylan travels his own road. He admits that his life is not a good example for kids to try and follow. In a way, his life has been that of a roving reporter, recording what he sees of his country.

He could have had yachts, Rolls Royces, or practically anything that money could buy, yet he preferred

Dylan is still a spellbinding songwriter and heartfelt singer, no matter what the music.

to tour the back roads. Dylan has spent much of his time looking at people and their lives. In a lazy sort of way, he has picked and chosen some of what he has seen and put it to music. Somehow, Bob Dylan has been able to bring people and messages to life in his songs.

Bob Dylan hasn't been hopping mindlessly from one thing to another. The messages he was sending out in his later, religion-inspired albums, such as *Slow Train Comin'*, weren't much different from his early days when he used religious images in songs such as "All Along the Watchtower." "You Gotta Serve Somebody," one of Dylan's earlier songs claimed. Thoughts about justice, freedom, and love have flown along with Bob Dylan from the days when he tried to collect from his father's customers in Hibbing. He has never stopped asking the important questions, and in doing so he has opened the way for others to do the same.

A Timeline of Bob Dylan's Life

May 24, 1941	Born in Duluth, Minnesota
1946	Family moves to Hibbing
June 1959	Graduates from high school
September 1959	Moves to Minneapolis to begin college at University of Minnesota
1959	Begins calling himself "Bob Dillon" at the coffeehouses near the University
Spring 1960	Drops out of the University; reads *Bound for Glory*, Woody Guthrie's autobiography
December 1960	Leaves for New York to see Woody
January 1961	Begins playing in coffeehouses in New York
February 1961	Meets Woody at a mutual friend's house
April 11, 1961	Opens in his first paying engagement in New York, at Gerde's Folk City
September 29, 1961	Glowing review of Dylan appears in *NY Times*; Dylan records backup on Carolyn Hester's album and is offered contract with Columbia Records
March 19, 1962	His first album, *Bob Dylan*, is released
August 9, 1962	Legally changes last name to Dylan
May 1963	*The Freewheelin' Bob Dylan* is released
May 18, 1963	Dylan plays at Monterey Folk Festival in California, his first real encounter with Joan Baez
June 18, 1963	"Blowin' in the Wind" is released by Peter, Paul and Mary—sells 320,000 copies in eight business days
July 1963	Plays for no fee at voter-registration rally in Greenwood, Mississippi
July 26-28, 1963	The Newport Folk Festival: Joan Baez has Bob sing with her, and he appears on stage four times during the Festival

51

August 28, 1963	Joins 200,000 others in the March on Washington in support of civil rights
August 1963	Joan Baez takes Bob on tour with her
October 1963	Flies parents to New York to see him in concert at Carnegie Hall
December 13, 1963	Receives Tom Paine Award, given by the Emergency Civil Liberties Committee to "someone who epitomizes the fight for freedom and equality"; his critical acceptance speech embarrasses both him and his hosts
February 1964	Goes on the road from New York to California through the Deep South; meets poet Carl Sandburg in North Carolina and plays concerts in Georgia, Mississippi, Colorado, and California
February 1964	*The Times They Are A-Changin'* is released
May 17, 1964	First tour of England begins with sold-out concert at Royal Festival Hall
July 1964	Appears at Newport Folk Festival
August 1964	*Another Side of Bob Dylan* is released
March 1965	The Byrds release "Mr. Tambourine Man"
March 1965	*Bringing It All Back Home* is released
April-June 1965	Tour of England is sold out within two hours; the documentary film *Don't Look Back* is filmed during the tour; the Beatles and the Rolling Stones come to the concert at Albert Hall
July 25, 1965	Appears with a rock band and electric guitar at Newport Folk Festival
August 28, 1965	Performs at Forest Hills Music Festival, Queens, NY; gets applause for acoustic set and gets boos and even fruit thrown at him for the electric songs
August 1965	*Highway 61 Revisited* is released
September 3, 1965 - December 15, 1965	Begins concert tour of U.S. and Canada, playing three or four shows a week, with rock band later known as The Band

November 22, 1965	Dylan marries Sara Lowndes, who has one daughter, Maria, by her first marriage
Sometime in 1966	Jesse Byron Dylan is born, the Dylans' first son
January 1966	Works on the *Blonde on Blonde* album
February 3, 1966 - May 7, 1966	Resumes concert tour with concerts in thirteen states and two Canadian provinces, then overseas to Australia, New Zealand, Scandinavia, Ireland, England, and France
May 1966	Returns to New York to hear that his manager has arranged for sixty-four more concerts in the U.S., starting immediately
May 1966	*Blonde on Blonde* is released
July 29, 1966	Motorcyle accident outside Woodstock; concerts are cancelled, a TV special for ABC's *Stage 67* is cancelled, and Dylan's book, *Tarantula*, is delayed
Sometime in 1967	Anna Dylan is born
March 1967	*Bob Dylan's Greatest Hits* is released
May 1967	The film of the 1965 British tour, *Don't Look Back*, is finally released
October 3, 1967	Woody Guthrie dies
January 20, 1968	Bob performs with many others at two "Tribute to Woody Guthrie" concerts; the money they raise goes to fight Huntington's chorea and to establish a library in Guthrie's home town
January 1968	*John Wesley Harding* is released
June 5, 1968	Bob's father dies and Bob returns to Hibbing for the funeral
July 1968	Seth Abraham Isaac Dylan is born
April 1969	*Nashville Skyline* is released
June 7, 1969	Appears on "The Johnny Cash Show" with Johnny Cash
August 31, 1969	Performs at Isle of Wight Festival with The Band
Late 1969	Samuel Dylan is born

June 1970	*Self Portrait* is released
June 9, 1970	Receives honorary doctorate of music degree from Princeton University
October 1970	*New Morning* is released
Spring 1971	Dylan's book, *Tarantula*, is finally published by Macmillan
May 1971	Visits Israel and stops by the Wailing Wall, an important religious symbol to Jews
August 1, 1971	Performs at the Concert for Bangladesh, a benefit for the victims of civil war and famine in Bangladesh
November 1971	*Bob Dylan's Greatest Hits Vol. II* is released
November 1972 - February 1973	On location in Durango, Mexico, filming *Pat Garrett and Billy the Kid*; records the soundtrack album in December
April 1973	First collection of song lyrics and poetry is published in *Writings and Drawings by Bob Dylan*
July 1973	*Pat Garrett and Billy the Kid* opens, soundtrack album is released
November 1973	*Dylan* is released
January 1974	*Planet Waves* is released
January 4, 1974	Begins another concert tour; receives over 5 million requests for the 650,000 available tickets in the tour; does forty concerts in six weeks in the U.S. and Canada
May 9, 1974	Performs at a "Friends of Chile" benefit concert for Chilean political refugees
June 1974	*Before the Flood* album, recorded during the 1974 tour, is released
January 1975	*Blood on the Tracks* is released
July 1975	*The Basement Tapes* is released; it was recorded in June-October 1967 at the house of a member of The Band, not intended for release. "Bootleg" (unauthorized) copies were being sold, so Dylan released his own version

54

October 31, 1975 - December 8, 1975	The Rolling Thunder Revue tour begins, with about 100 people including musicians (Joan Baez among them), lighting technicians, advance men, road crew, and so forth
January 1976	*Desire* is released
April 18, 1976 - May 26, 1976	Rolling Thunder Revue tour resumes; one show was taped and broadcast later on NBC-TV
September 1976	*Hard Rain* is released
November 1976	Appears at The Band's last concert at Winterland Palace in San Francisco, which was made into the movie *The Last Waltz*
November 1976	*The Songs of Bob Dylan from 1966 through 1975* is published
1977	*Renaldo and Clara*, a film based on the Rolling Thunder Revue tour, is released
June 28, 1977	Bob and Sara divorce
February 20, 1978 - November 23, 1978	Concert tour of ten countries; some say he has "gone Vegas" because he has three backup singers and a larger band
June 1978	*Street-Legal* is released
Early 1979	Dylan experiences "a vision and feeling," in which the room he is in actually moves, and he "accepts Jesus Christ into his life"
August 1979	*Slow Train Coming* is released, the first of the religious trilogy
October 1979 - December 1979	Plays only his religious music at all U.S. concerts, even though he is booed
February 27, 1980	Wins first Grammy award for "Gotta Serve Somebody" off his *Slow Train* album, and accepts it in white tie and tuxedo
April-May 1980	Plays thirty U.S. concerts, still only gospel music
June 1980	*Saved* is released, the second in the trilogy
November 1980	At concerts in San Francisco, begins to sing older, non-religious songs again
June-July 1981	Concert tour of England

August 1981	*Shot of Love* is released, last of the religious trilogy
November 1983	*Infidels* is released, not a religious album
Summer 1984	Another European concert tour
December 1984	*Real Live* is released
January 1985	Participates in "We Are the World" recording for USA for Africa
June 1985	*Empire Burlesque* is released
July 13, 1985	Appears at Live Aid concert to benefit African famine victims, and mentions in passing that musicians should do a benefit for American farmers
September 22, 1985	Appears at Farm Aid concert at University of Illinois in Champaign
Fall 1985	*Lyrics, 1962-1985* by Bob Dylan is published
November 1985	*Biograph* is released
July 1986	*Knocked Out Loaded* is released

56

J B DYLAN
Aaseng, Nathan.
Bob Dylan, spellbinding
songwriter $7.95

52427